To my grandchildren, Niyah, JR, Pooh, Boo, and Sugga. You can be all that God would have you to be. Put God first in everything you do.
I Love you!

-MA 'MA

Ordering Information:
For details, contact- mattiedlide@yahoo.com
Hardback ISBN: 979-8-9863605-1-5
Paperback ISBN: 979-8-9863605-2-2
eBook ISBN: 979-8-9863605-3-9

I am who GOD says I am

WRITTEN BY MATTIE STEWART

ILLUSTRATED BY TRAVIS A. THOMPSON

I AM KIND

AND BE KIND TO ONE ANOTHER, TENDERHEARTED, FORGIVING ONE ANOTHER, EVEN AS GOD IN CHRIST FORGAVE YOU.

EPHESIANS 4:32

I AM
POWERFUL

BEHOLD, I HAVE GIVEN YOU AUTHORITY TO TREAD ON SERPENTS AND SCORPIONS, AND OVER ALL THE POWER OF THE ENEMY, AND NOTHING SHALL HURT YOU.

LUKE 10:19

I AM
WONDERFULLY
MADE

I WILL PRAISE YOU, FOR I AM FEARFULLY AND WONDERFULLY MADE.
PSALMS 139:14

I AM
OBEDiENT

"CHILDREN, OBEY YOUR PARENTS IN THE LORD, FOR THIS IS RIGHT".
EPHESIANS 6:1

GROCERY

I AM
LOVED

WE LOVE HIM BECAUSE HE
FIRST LOVED US.

1 JOHN 4:19

GOD LOVES ME!

I AM
CONFiDENT

I CAN DO ALL THINGS THROUGH CHRIST
WHO STRENGTHENS ME.

PHILIPPIANS 4:13

I AM
RIGHTEOUS

FOR HE MADE HIM WHO KNEW NO SIN TO BE SIN FOR US, THAT WE MIGHT BECOME THE RIGHTEOUSNESS OF GOD IN HIM.

2 CORINTHIANS 5:21

I AM SMART

THE FEAR OF THE LORD IS THE BEGINNING OF WISDOM: AND THE KNOWLEDGE OF THE HOLY ONE IS GOOD UNDERSTANDING.

PROVERBS 9:10

A+

I AM
A CHILD OF
GOD

BUT AS MANY AS RECEIVED HIM, TO THEM HE GAVE THE RIGHT TO BECOME CHILDREN OF GOD, TO THOSE WHO BELIEVE IN HIS NAME.

JOHN 1:12

Mattie Stewart is a Charlotte, North Carolina Transportation bus driver, and previously worked as an assistant teacher. She worked in the school system for 20 plus years. There she worked with children of all ages. She has three children of her own and five grandchildren. Her heart is with children and she wants to encourage children to be all that they can be!